THE WARHOL PILLOWS

poems by

Diane Wald

Finishing Line Press
Georgetown, Kentucky

THE WARHOL PILLOWS

ACKNOWLEDGMENTS

Annus Miserabilis and *Echolocation* appeared in New World Writing
What She Said, When She Sat Up appeared in the American Poetry Review
L as in Labyrinth appeared in Provincetown Arts
I Like the Little Rocket Ships appeared in Ecopoetry
faustinetta, gegenschein, trapunto appeared in the chapbook *faustinetta, gegenschein, trapunto* (Cervena Barva Press)
my trip to iceland and *pluperfect* appeared in 5Trope
It's Just the Noise of the Water and *My Undertaker Wears a Sweet Cologne*
    appeared in The Laurel Review
It Seems as if a Combination of Consonants... appeared in The Dalhousie
    Review

Publisher: Leah Huete de Maines
Editor: Christen Kincaid
Cover Art: Robert Wald
Author Photo: Diane Wald
Cover Design: Elizabeth Maines McCleavy

Order online: www.finishinglinepress.com
        also available on amazon.com

Author inquiries and mail orders:
Finishing Line Press
P. O. Box 1626
Georgetown, Kentucky 40324
U. S. A.

Table of Contents

for Carey

L AS IN LABYRINTH

black nights, white peonies,
and the olives: castelvetrano, mantequilla, cerignola.

it may never happen to me again,
that which i loved so much.

the sunset's starting early,
violet pink outside the doctor's office window.
he knows people i know yet somehow
i trust him with my secrets

as if we were lovers, or even as if
we were strolling rhode island again

like two people who could not die.

CONCOCTED BECAUSE OF THE JOURNALS OF JOAN MIRÓ

I must begin by thanking you
with all my heart. Tillya has already finished
the portrait of Branch and me, and I am
working furiously; I am working on figures
and still lifes—what Manuel calls my period
of formal concentration. Does the enthusiasm
of Manuel surprise you? Despite
differences in personality and background,
we are becoming lifelong friends.

You ask
about the south: it was a true assassination
of painting; secrets
were lost and found again
through my father's science and intuition. Around that time
my life began to change
for the better. I invented "The Song
of the Vowels." And so I began to draw. Yet the usual
walk through the public gardens, which normally
offers rare insight, is suddenly in need
of verbal accompaniment. Won't you please
come see me? The whole organization of society,
a pointy pattern based on a rubbed green background,
repeats that we certainly must explore
all the golden sparks of our souls.

On the other hand, it's not hard for me to tell you
where those other figures come from. It's the material
that decides, but Oliver says that he questions
the material. If you come here, I will allow you
to sleep all day. But I digress from Oliver's story: in January
he decided to spend more time in Spain; he bought a house
and a plot of land and a parrot and a grievous
grey boyfriend. Upon arrival, he sent to Paris for the crates
of the process of self-examination. He was removed

from the frenetic social activity
of that particular musical lavender of France.

But now I am thinking of something violent, like falling
ice or falling words—something human. And of the time
you used the expression "port-cochère." Below,
as you begged me, I have listed
all of the paintings executed
during the wine-drenched years. Do you remember
Vandalia, as I do? If I couldn't afford the train,
she would slip me a little money. Once,
in order to get her franc's worth,
I went as far as Russia. But alas now I am convinced
I only owe lip service
to a certain big heart, and really no
personality—I always
look ahead and she looks back.

So engagingly I have recounted all of this
just for you, my beloved —and, I think—in fact I am sure
—if you die,
I will be frightened right out of my wits.

BIG BEETLE

He must have flown into the porch light last night and this morning was lying on his back on the green step. Poor scarab. *He's beautiful* is what C said and he was: the size of a thimble and cocoa brown with black spots. And that fabulous scarab-face, inscrutable and kind. The Dalai Lama, in a way, and I don't think he would mind. We weren't sure it was a male scarab, of course, but it seemed like one somehow, the way certain things seem male and others female, and no matter how you fight it, you don't know why.

PEONIES LARGE AND FRAGRANT

Inside the garden in front of the house
last year's snail shells crackle under foot.

Can you tell me that story again,
the one where we meet in the garden?

Delphinium rise like periscopes
from an ocean of gold coreopsis.

I have hidden five pennies for you
between rocks near the dark lobelia.

New cherries blush and ripen
on branches we thought had been broken.

The woman who comes here to pray
is wearing your favorite epaulettes.

I will not tell you again
what I have not told you before.

You're alive inside me like lights,
like lights that are stars in my forehead.

My flowers rise up each spring no matter what I do;
my life grows thicker no matter how much you have stolen.

PLUPERFECT

did you die before the end of the world
and did you die by bomb?

if otherwise, kindly tell us
how you died
because we are hurtling toward death
with very few maps to guide us
the dead are waiting
for us to catch up

i was hitchhiking, i was
dreaming of the pearl
whether you believe it or not she said
whether you believe

whether you wear the ring or bracelet
or keep the pearl in your head

and then she was gone, disappearing down
an infinite staircase
where i refused to follow

in the field a palomino fox
paler than we'd imagined, practically
floating on air she was so pale
last season's hibiscus
stranded in the lanai
and pallbearers unexpectedly requested
to pick up the slack
to tote their passive burden

"life," she said
"got that outta my system"
she had married a cryptozoologist
who considered her extinct and presented her
with a miner's light
to wear on her easter hat

to cover all contingencies
he said "i was born with a head outside my heart,
and cannot correct it"

and she?
she had been rushed through childhood

she certainly wasn't in any hurry now

SNOW ON A VELVET CLOCHE

I am about to see the film
everyone else has seen.
No, it is not death.
Death is not in this story.
I am not about to behold the birds of my body
wander into night forgetting about their wings,
ambling stupidly on matchstick legs
with their rhinestone eyes rolling
— no!
Most of those little birds can still fly.
I go to the movies.

I wait in my seat without removing hat or scarf.
I wait, in fact, feeling a little cold.
My fingers cling to a paper cup of coffee
like a beggar's to her bowl. The theater's full.
The people around me are all in love,
the women's hair electrified from their showers,
showers taken before lovemaking or after,
and the men are all gentle with them, leaning over
to perfect each laugh they share, to tame the hair,
to cover each hand. To inhale.

This film is a classic
I have always missed. I know its melodies.
Like many I have aped the dress of its actress.
Sometimes I hear its dialogue
just as I fall to a dream
and I fall then like the most brittle of trees
to a dream that is classic and ill-remembered.
Today I will finally see the film.
The film is not love; it is not remembrance.

This particular print has aged;
I know that though the film has not started.
A certain rasp and hesitation,
an endearing lack of synchronization,

these things and the inevitable grainy silk
of faces washed overboard—for this I am waiting.
The happiness of waiting is mine; I am
a living lace of nerves, perspiring now,
as the curtain starts to slide and the lights grow dimmer,
and the lovers around me loosen their embraces.
The coffee is forgotten, the hat slides from my ears.
I am afraid now; I am so afraid—
alone. That's it. I'm the only one here

the only one here on the ceiling, flying solo.
Over the tender exit an oval blue light glows.

THIS WINTER

As soon as one salmon velvet petal drifts away
from the peace rose in the side garden
I understand
that this time the seasons are really changing.

I am married to a man as tall as the Empire State Building
and as wide.
When we go out, he takes my arm
as if to say don't
go without me.

We're all going this time. The earth groans under
the weight of our folly: leaves, lives, liberties
shifted off balance, teetering in grief
like swallows fallen ill midair, surprised that anything
could stop them.

YOU'RE THERE

Again in the dream it's William Hurt, again in a vest, this time buttoned high and *ha* I say I know *what you stand for this time, it's your name, something's* <u>hurt</u> *me, that's it, right?* And also, I think to myself, very cunningly, I also know he *looks like* somebody else, the character in that movie for example, and even he no doubt stood for somebody else so I'm in no danger of this being *really* William Hurt, although I do think he's a wonderful actor, but it isn't him in this dream. And I lean up against this isn't-him-in-the-dream and put my arms around him and he's a little surprised but he holds me so tenderly, unexpectedly, (I guess I didn't think he was like that) and he's very, very glad to see me, and has this kind of wonderful unstated humorous accepting *knowledge* of me and it turns me on. He is listening listening listening, and it's just about everything I ever wanted, but there's more, there's a reading in the dream, a poetry reading at great bookstore where everyone sits around a huge round table eating what looks like some kind of spinach tart, and coffee of course, very good dark coffee, maybe hazelnut, and anyhow they love me there and the proprietor of the store, a dark little man who also looks like somebody else—I can't think who—says they've been waiting for me for fifty years. That's really good, I think, and I look all around: William Hurt isn't there anymore but you are.

STREET: A WALK OF BARELY FIVE MINUTES

In the west tree of love (this being
the past) a singing bird dies, the flame
mistreated in its body like this character I admire
in a piece of fiction, the one who is strong and
racked and proud, plain but impassioned and so much
like the self each of us wants
that the east tree seems nearer (it being
future and dear). My room
grew colder; therefore, more
clear, the rusted doorknob finally crumbled off
and a sullen, very shy noun stunned all of us.
The streets have engagements of their own
as particles of them are carried off
on the feet of the wanderer. Let me now speak
of a deaf happiness the wanderer had
that year; his large hat bloomed, his wife
owned new utensils, yet here he is today
at the gate of the underground selling
"valentine flowers." The week is wrong
and the surface of the street just above him
roughens a little, just
a bit. Stepping with some lost pain,
I think of this: thick tape
around doors, a memory of what was down
that other street, how quickly one could slouch
into complaisant knowledge of those trees, his
chest, the ignorant unreal stars. We met
in unbound gold that time,
the wanderer on his way
to where I had had just been: exceptional day! For just
three moments we grew so warm
my hairline began to imitate coastal lines:
the wanderer had undressed before the dawn
and shillied off and clambered down
the narrowing field until his figure pawned
all likeness to itself. His throat in the sun
survives: all tragedies

of ultimate greatness are unknown. Say he was one
who practiced understatement upon
his companion.

WIDOW WIDOW

give it all
and it will be taken away

doubtless

she who speaks with her whole body
hears the silence

even in the garden
where the strangest frond

veers up from the earth
unleashing bells of amber

who planted this and would she ever
do it again?

THIS TIME

day to day
little changes toward death
don't notice us
or we them

then an oriole flies
into our window
and for a single reason
our bones jangle

it's nothing we say
as the bird flies away
the bird was not harmed
this time

FAUSTINETTA

1.

my hair blew backwards over my head as i talked to the llamas.
now that i see the photograph i wonder where is that green shirt?

things are better now, though not perfect.

not that i expect perfection. not that i resent
the perfection i expected in the past. not
that the perfection is your lie, although your lie
is near perfection.

faustinetta looks up the word "natufian" because it appears
in a weblog about her cousin's former husband's present wife
who makes big paintings. he is a dowser. the natufians

may have lived in underground houses, and a natufian male,
aged 25-30, may have been buried with a tender arm
slung around his dog.

but when and how did that dog die? another
illusion of tenderness. i work too much
near the source of pain. you are the falling

floaters in my eye, my left eye.
they proceed from right to left from bottom to top
illogically. sometimes i fear them. they seem like
precursors.

"i want to see the fox but the fox is not forthcoming"

my husband says she only comes on wednesdays

2.

we sat in the car and you told me that as a child
your mother had forced you to smell something foul

somehow i cannot believe it

it was an ice-cold night. i had to swathe myself
from head to toe in flannels
i had to disguise my face

with enormous eyeglasses stolen from a corpse

i had to drive through treacherous ice-storms into your neighborhood
where only the ice-cold headlights of oncoming cars
buoyed my obsession

in one car i thought i saw your mother
as the headlights moved around the corner

i was blinded. i heard a voice
say *this and only this*

was it the voice
of a misogynist?

3.

i am a sick woman
i have lost my pen top
i have misplaced the beginning
of my flash drive
i find myself reaching for names
the apocryphal gospels have all but deleted
i am studying meridian points
and tapping to correct them
there's a haze in the yard but no foxes
still no foxes yet
how can you universally uncatgorically misinterpret
my every word

i am a sick woman perhaps

but i have my standards

4.

maybe nobody's asked you.
i'd like to ask you.
what's it like?

to have that kind of sound come out of you?
when do you work on that hobby of yours?

all the women you have lied to.

all the calming influences that proceed from those lies.

all the smooth kisses and near misses and couch conversations.

we are so tired of it.

5.

i am ever so slightly in love you know
                              (little tiny teeth)
i would not say i am proud of this new problem
                              (capillaries bending)
i can hear things through my central ear i could not hear before
                              (piles of sumo fat)
                              (glorious wizardry)
at least it has gotten me off of my ass

6.

i am pretty darn psychic today. i'm all revved up. i am doing okay.

i walked upstairs to see my friend j. just as she was writing me an email.

she looked amazed. i'm not sure why.

lurex spandex gold lamé
"geisha" means "art-person." yes that's right

your autobiography guided by dusky lanterns
the coded episodes of agency and communion
sequences of redemption and quizzical hoodwinkery
contamination of self by self by self

i wanted to take your head between my hands
and forcefully insert a metaphor that would bind you to the truth

i wanted to smash your towers of pomp and pleasantry
and give you a lung to smoke, a heart to attack, an appendix to index

i cannot find you

INTERVIEW WITH LISP

For my happiness I am not loved.
One cannot expect it.
In my youth I wore silver hose and buds,
I wakened early, I opened triangular windows.

In the cool sky over Arkansas,
I saw a rose etched in the sky.
The smallest airplanes were elegant,
lifting achingly off the fields along the river.

I discovered my head in a basket fashioned of hands.
I see you never, never dance the way
my flamenco idol buttons up his shoe.

Tonight has nearly fallen off the spoon.

THE MOCK TURTLENECK IS A DIFFICULT ITEM TO WEAR

He said, "At one time you suffered a terrible joie de vivre," and I knew it was true.
I needed to get back there.

The humming did confuse me, though it was only in certain type of light.
I knew I was supposed to ignore it.

She had pickles in her car, the report divulged, and this was not deemed
    to be unusual.
My brother is becoming a gumshoe.
He freely admits this.

And I wanted the summer to back off a little, to stop burning trees.
All over the yard things browned to a thoughtful crisp.

My eyelids kept falling and sleep was a mottled flower. Formerly I had ridden sleep
to the sun.

I knew it would be hard, but not this easy.
Recently this one dog made me reconsider.

THE SECRET OF THE FAILURE

is to use the failure. The hawk falls
but you have not seen it, tell me
it wasn't a
hawk. I try
but fail
to sustain the vision. The secret

of the failure is to use
the failure. I call you and you are stuck
in the center of a zinnia, the tight petals
enfolding you,
the mossy scent
enveloping you, the sizz of the bees
deafening you; you cannot
hear me, hear
that I'm failing. The voice
on the answering machine at night
is a zinnia, nothing
more.

The secret
of the failure is to use
the failure. Your sickness,
mother,
it comes and it goes. You're like a walnut,
cracked unevenly,
and left too long in the shell. When you're well
you want all the doors open. And yet I cannot

walk in. The secret of the failure is
to use the failure.

BIRTHDAY

Yet another holiday and you present me with a cake of ice, a sixteen-by-sixteen inch cube, tied like a box of chocolates with a thick satin ribbon. The ribbon is blue. I pull on one end of the bow and the ribbon comes loose in one swift fall; it's that nicely made. Who wrapped this? I embrace the cube. I thank you. I freeze to death.

WHAT SHE SAID, WHEN SHE SAT UP

Early this morning,
when you could not touch me,
I had a dream the great doctors took hold of my heart,
evicted it from me, stitched me together,
and listened while I narrated, amazed, composed, elated,
the tale of this my bloodless
and spiritless surrender.

The dream was a grand dream
illustrated in moonlight.
My legs swam out from a green coverlet
like the uncovered roots
of a stream-teased tree.
You could not touch me.
The dream was my compensation.

Previously it seems I had been waltzing with my father.
The lame swore at me
and the lame were lame no longer.
It was a beautiful dream
as you slept so still beside me.
It was like helping a blind woman
over a high, sharp stone.

The great doctors operate without anesthesia.
It is often permissible
to keep on one's clothes.
They are men and women, they are novices and ancients,
all of them working magically and quickly,
each of them meticulous and kind and how astonished
was I, as I lay there, counting backwards, counting forwards,
to observe the wedding bands they so stylishly wore
over their surgical gloves
with no fear of contamination.

The dream was so sexy
my hair began to wander.

I had the sensation
I was making a tall man laugh.
I had the eerie feeling
a naked man lay beside me
also offering up his heart
to the sweet deliverance,
and yet only the knives had touched me,
the swift obedient knives.

I remember thinking of vodka then in the dream,
of the liquor like water tumbling over and over the ice,
of the taste that is not a taste, the taste that is satisfaction,
that takes getting used to, that is foreign, familiar, wise,
that tastes like a man to a woman,
that tastes like a woman to a man.

Just before sleeping
my heart had rattled and shattered.
Now without that heart
I was electrified.
I knew I would have a zipper scar
to be smoothed away by a lover's hands.
Or perhaps it was that heart-shaped space inside me
I wanted him to fill
that drove me mad.

The dream went on for hours
while you did not know I was sleeping.
In the dream you touched me so tenderly
that the moon arose golden
and broken china mended.
In the dream I lived in your pocket
and you lived in the edges of my eyes.
You looked on in the dream as the doctors cured me.
You cried out against them, you seemed to be weeping.
In the dream I was perfected,
I was what I'd always wanted.

I considered that you'd been perfected too,
but I felt no true pain, love,
I felt no real desire.

CHANNELING

It comes to me from somewhere else, I don't know where. I don't know who sent it.

It is rich with detail.

I suspect the sender is someone I want to know, someone I once knew. I think he is dead now. He contacts me. He contacted me years ago.

He tells me the story of the young man with wheels for arms. He tells me the story of the young man

who killed him. He remembers things about me. I am older now than he ever got to be.

I am older now than my father ever got to be. I wonder what he would've been like as an old man. Would we have argued again? About the deer.

Would we have liked each other? Would I have liked him better than I liked my mother?

The man who sends me stories is now is not my father, never was. He was a lover sometimes. He was

an avenue to the endless ocean of the unseen.

THE WARHOL PILLOWS

In Spain, in Altea, you broke down. Why
I remember this today

twirling in the gallery full of floating
helium-filled silver pillows

isn't really amazing. And after
you take my picture, you and I

have a photo-strip taken by the machine
in the basement of the Warhol Museum

and lo and behold we are happy,
our own true selves, our radiant faces

crowded together in black and white
show a fierce youth hidden

by the colors of passing days. Never
am I happier than when

surrounded by silver clouds; never are you better
than behind your camera,

recording my bliss, honing in
on the unseen nugget of my being

that without the camera you cannot glimpse
or touch, and who knows why. In Altea

you broke down, and credited me
with salvation, but today

it's Andy who plays savior
as we wait for ourselves on the concrete steps

in this his fashionable city, where everything shines

with a clip from some honest and crazy film

where people say just what they mean
without realizing what they are doing.

WHAT HAPPENED TO ME LAST NIGHT

not in london
but in a suburb of myself
not where the land trips the sea or vice versa
but inside the inside
on the leg of a flying wasp

better than the shadow you left, more rocky
longer than your prayer, since you told no truths
in the shy eye, the too-fast heart, the heart fasting

later you'll arrive
later

the bedsprings rust
something dies near the dumpster
was it animalvegetablemineral

you'll get no twenty questions
you'll arrive at age with a spoon in your handbag
you'll never get through the screening

last night i crept into the building in full sight
i was not hidden, but invisible
you knew me

THREE

1.
This morning it remains unclear
whether the crisis will be averted by continual assault
with imaginary or real medication of the preventive sort
or whether a visit will have to be made
to several tired physicians
of body and soul. The mind
does not seem to enter into it
any more than it did yesterday
when she observed three men
constructing a fieldstone wall: one, highly muscled,
carting fieldstones from another pile
closer to the second, who slathered each selection
with a dollop of gray mortar, placing each
atop the next with such extraordinary care
the mortar could not be seen from across the road—or even
a few feet away—and the casual observer would begin to wonder
whether the stones had simply fallen somehow
into this wondrous heap, although of course that would never
seem true. The third man stood
a little apart, watching with that careful attention
that could only bespeak a hidden love. The second man, once
in a while, chipped off a corner of stone
from a piece that did not quite fit. Then he went on. Clearly he did not care
for one stone more than another.

2.
In another sense, in another time, a first man did not think
a second man "his type." (The wives
of these two were friends.) This was not a romantic
assessment; rather, the first attempted to appease
what he felt to be almost an irrational need
on the part of him and his wife
to make sense of things. The second man
had accused the wife of the first
of something untoward—they did not speak of it
after the first discussion, wherein the second man

confronted the first man's wife with his, shall we say, unusual
idea. After that (and it was left
that the second man wasn't fully satisfied
he was mistaken, although the wife made all valiant attempts
to continue normally, except in her disgust
when the second man later offered his cheek to be kissed) nothing
was spoken, except of course by the wife
to the first man, her mate, who was shocked and
dismayed. At first, however,
he was only surprised; it was later dismay set in,
and he wondered whether some confrontation on his part
shouldn't be initiated with the second man,
whom unfortunately he had already somewhat
disliked. The first man's wife
was truly valiant, as I have said,
but suffered nonetheless, and she in her turn wondered
whether the second man had accused her in some attempt
to separate the affections of her and her man, or even to come between her
and the second man's wife, a confidant
for years. Summer holidays
were coming, and no one knew
quite what to do.

3.
Whether to hold on to the third cat was the question, and one
that raised others. Was it possible
to integrate someone new
into an already existing and highly successful (even
on the emotional front, in
its way) scenario, or would it be better to find the third cat a home
where he could start afresh as leader of his own
territory? Certainly
he deserved the best, as he had shown them
only sweetness and a creative
intelligence so far. And another concern: since he was not
fully grown, might he not grow into
something—either habit-wise or even

in his bones—not as agreeable to all as he was agreeable
now? Would the first two residents
be jealous? Angry? Hurt? Would
there be, in perpetuity,
exactly enough food, water, love
to go around? It was never
as easy as it seemed that day
when he first came crying to the door.

YOU MUST SAY SOMETHING NOW

I tie up and stake the poppies, the peonies,
whatever columbine
still stand (blue and white especially
fragile in this wind), arrange
long legs of clematis
along the mailbox fence, bug-dust
the echinacea, weed around
basil and daisies, poke in the dirt
where I thought those tall bells
would be returning, pinch off
purple petunias, re-seed
the sunflower bed, fall back on my heels
and rest. A man walks by
and smiles, says I'm doing a good job. He has
a southern accent, and on a cool day
in June in Massachusetts
it sounds like honey. He says down South
they like beautiful things. I remember
I have to tell you
something. I remember
to put the trowel away. I remember
the way you looked at me twice
with your wide wide eyes this morning.

GEGENSCHEIN

*"You, your joys and your sorrows, your memories and your ambitions,
your sense of personal identity and free will, are in fact no more
than the behavior of a vast assembly of nerve cells and their associated
molecules."* Frances Crick, *The Astonishing Hypothesis*

For days we noticed the fullness of the moon. We had reached, I thought,
a peaceful place,
and both of us were contented. Sentences
finished themselves without interruption,
most of the time. On the way to the station one morning
C. told me how once, as a child,
he sang "Paper Moon" to a roomful of grownups (including a monsignor),
but did not understand the words. "Hanging over a cardboard sea"
was especially confusing to him,
until years later.

I was reading a book about ensoulment, not strictly.
A psychic in the book identified
a woman's brother's hourglasses, which
he collected. For this reason the woman was convinced
of the psychic's credibility.
There was a great deal of talk about the discarnate,
and how we might—and they might—
commune with each other.
I was glad I had taken Latin
for four years.

Nobody. No
body.

I came across *gegenschein*, defined as a "faint oval patch of light
directly opposite the sun in the night sky, caused by reflection of sunlight
by dust particles—also known as
counterglow." I found this hard
to picture. It's different from zodiacal light, which is vaguely triangular,
but has colors identical to those
of that solar spectrum. (Suddenly I remembered

how long we sat on the airport floor while waiting
for that flight. Suddenly I remembered
walking in that forest in Maine,
carrying umbrellas.) The sometimes oval gegenschein is
a much fainter spot of light.

Radiational backscattering! The apparent cause of gegenschein. The wavelengths
are reflected backwards
so much better than in all other directions. Several Italians,
in the remarkable year 2000
carried heavy astronomical equipment
to the top of Stromboli (in a continuous state of eruption
for 2000 years), and positioned themselves near the cemetery
to observe the gegenschein. It was a perfect night
with almost no wind at all, and they confirmed
that Stromboli has one of the darkest skies in Europe. I was pleased
to wake up to find
that C. had brought a stunned woodcock
up to our hotel room
on the 20th floor.

He'd found it in the street, preposterously.
The bird rested calmly
in the purple lining of C's jacket
for some time. Then it began to fly; I had to confine it
in a towel. C. freed it
in the park, although alas,
we believed it too invisibly wounded
to survive. All day I scanned
the painted window screens of Baltimore
for images of falling birds. (I remembered the silver Icarus
in the museum,
surrounded by windows. I remembered the still-life painter from Delft
and his trademark red spittoon.)

From a seismic point of view, we were in a state
of persistent volcanic tremor. I had not thought of it

myself. I did consider
something like it when reminded
of 17th century *tulipomania*, which is just what it sounds like:
Europe's obsession with tulips,
undoubtedly an unhealthy preoccupation.
I have no idea
what that did to the birds.

Or whether the tulips had been ensouled
to the point that they thought about haunting
in later centuries.
I felt as if I were standing in the inkwell.
I remembered a painting called *Duel after Masquerade,*
in which a clown stood sadly gazing at a pistol
while another man in costume was carried away. I remembered

the counter man in the Roly Poly Sandwich Shoppe
telling us he was 37 and had been married 15 years
and had a daughter not from this marriage
but "from a young lady I met in college," and he
[later I hear him while I'm waiting for our rollups with artichoke hearts]
is worried that another young lady [a customer, I gather]
who is married as he is married has not only been talking to him
"too much" but has somehow appeared—twice—at the same bus stop he uses
on his way home.
He's worried about this, he tells his friend,
"so I go home a different way."
I searched for my ectoplasm
in order to wear it home.

And finally I found it.
The trains were confusing for us, we had been through so much.
And yet in a certain way there was no strain at all.

DON AND THE FAMILY MATTER

Mother was a registered nurse on private duty. In the town next-door, where Richard Nixon once lived for a time, she spent many months caring for a man who lived in a big ritzy house with his wife and a small beige dog, which Mother described as "barky." Instead of getting well or dying, as most of Mother's patients did, this man kept getting sicker. The doctors ordered, as they are fond of saying, "every conceivable test," but they could not find out why the man wouldn't get well. His name was probably Don. Of course this was easily fifty years ago or more. There's nothing on the internet. Anyway it turned out he was being slowly poisoned by a family member. It put him in a wheelchair before anyone solved the conundrum. I was told he kept a silver pitcher of water by his bed and wore plaid Bermuda shorts when he was able. Not sure if he played golf before he got ill, but probably. Did the little beige dog jump up in anyone's lap? Also not sure. The wife was not the guilty party, but it was a family matter. A nephew perhaps. Or perhaps it is always easier to blame the nephew in a town where Richard Nixon used to live.

ANNUS MISERABILIS

It was the year Peter O'Toole died,
but that wasn't the worst of it.

Everything scared me,
yet I was brave.

My house demanded
I take a vow of silence.

I dreamed of a man on a bus
who said I would never survive.

One rock in our yard was perpetually moist
in spite of the terrible drought.

I could always see through you,
but I would not look.

The red tree died.
The blue tree died.

Poems that once made me happy
made me happy no more.

When I closed my eyes
I could still see billows of lava.

Worse, though, were the drunks confessing
their drunkenness to the wind.

And worst of all my elegiac swan
transgressing my veins like a white drug in autumn.

CAMELLIA WOMAN (I RECALL HOPE WHEN IT LAST APPEARED)

Even in the stretched heat
of that August day
I was able to feel it, pulsing
like a huge,
able
artery. Even
though you'd moved me like a pawn
through an afternoon of rigid
conversation. Even
though my hair, melted by the sea
air, stuck
to my shoulders,
and my cotton dress clung
only to me
like a thin paste of flowers.
Even when the answers I gave
couldn't find
any questions. Even when Bad
Someone called with Bad News
and the weather grew warmer
even than we'd dreaded. Even when
I lay awake at two,
and half of two
killed me. Even
in the sad mosquito night
as your breathing stopped and started
and you gave me
no room. Even the snow,
a dream I hated,
seemed welcome to me then.

The last tiger
didn't stop me, as it did so often,
lurking in Asian forests,
waiting to die. Even though the earth
spun backward

for one moment,
and the strange African spider spit a web like a dropcloth
over its victim,
even then,
even then.

IT'S JUST THE NOISE OF THE WATER SEEPING THROUGH THE HARDENED GROUND

I locked my radio in the desk drawer and it kept on playing for sixteen years. Remember the psychiatrist who had a model of a ship in his therapy room? Nothing like that. Everything I said had been proven false, but the jury still heard it. I had fallen down the stairs but I did not die and I was not buried. But therefore I know. It was that time of winter when the towels get wild just by being in the house. If I could I would steal cakes off the tea tray, while the wonders of the world returned slowly, one by one. My moss intended to enjoy itself every day, in spite of the maddening drip-drip-drip you could hear from the ruined four-poster as well as the driveway.

CUBA

I have carried the heaviest objects to the porch,
Applied oil and musk; I have threaded the anxious needle
And am prepared. To think I should have to travel, unable
To paint, to dream these flounces ever again.

As the evening grins white odors from the shore
it erases the marks of the sand from the sleeper's cheek.
The treacheries then become easier to see,
bobbing along the waves, electrocuted birds.

I will cease correcting love. I will watch you when I can.
Whatever you have not told me will be that gift
between surface and depth, boundary and boundary.
The later the meals, the less often I will go hungry.

MY UNDERTAKER WEARS A SWEET COLOGNE

I mean, I like it. He gets up close to you, real close—he has to. It's his job. You know he's probably going to say you belong under ground, but it's not the man's fault, not at all. Better him than some others I can think of. And if you're not dead you don't have to listen to him anyway, but just in case. The only advice he ever gave me was "never give a dog a tomato," but he didn't explain why. He looks like the kind of guy who has a falsetto. Not that he uses it, just that he has one. And if you ask him too many questions he will tell you he's been exhausted by the surreal that day and will have to get back to you. And he will. He's a gentleman after all, and I suspect a bit sad but not depressed. I glimpsed the inside of his Audi: filled with clouds. Last year he fell in love with and married one of his clients. He's a great guy.

DIVORCE

My husband goes sailing
in the living room
every night.
He has constructed
a makeshift boat shell
in which he sits
blasting music so loud through his headphones
that I cannot sleep
even rooms away.

He sits there
pretending he's on the sea
learning to lean and work the sails
so that if he ever
gets out there
he'll know how to do it.

If only
he'd pretend
that he knew how to live with me.

TRAPUNTO

1.
in a repressed society there will be a lot of silence because silence is contagious and if you're not
allowed to say certain things eventually you won't want to say others either and there won't be a
lot of good things said

g said

"i really like potatoes" or

"of course you like potatoes"

it was a joke between us

then he slipped in "i'm never going
to get well"

and i remembered j had said something like that to me years ago
as he served the tea
sweet tea in big glass mugs

in *trapunto* the design is outlined with two or more rows of running stitches and then padded
from the underside to achieve a raised effect

here's what i remember of his story

he was a genius child
he picked up broken pieces of glass and fashioned them into trees
ghosts followed him around with baskets to pick up genius words
he might let fall
somebody loved him
but ignorantly

was it a dream i had NO
not a dream

trapunto with his head in his hands a headache
the headache a trapeze on which he walked unsteadily falling

fall into my arms trapunto fall into my arms

it's all coming back in a rush

the kiss at the door that wasn't a kiss at the door
my scarlet sweater
the kiss just inside the door when the sky/clouds/ceiling fell in
accounting for trapunto's headache

he showed me his pain machine
his anti-pain machine
you stare into it and go off above your mind hypnotically
and the pain goes elsewhere

he took care the pain did not go into me

i brushed my hair

2.

much to my amazement
a tight elastic hairnet of pain (of stars)
was pulled down tightly over your skull

i shouldn't have told you what i was thinking
it was this

one could take the wind and wind it around missing persons all over the world and
find them
if one were on speaking terms with the wind
considering that the persons wanted to be found
(there will always be some who do not)

just before the bridge over the wide salty water there is a store

in which you can buy soda for missing persons and photographs of yourself
in a lobby machine
for them to remember you by

you can send these
via e-mail
all in one smooth transaction
except for the sodas

i am not speaking of persons in memory
or persons with orange hats or persons necessarily who
are not yet born
or are choosing not to be born or not to die

i am talking about the hairnet of pain that some people endure
that trapunto endured
the tight elastic dark blue navy blue hairnet of stars pulled down over the head
bespeaking unendurable pain for some people

however beautiful
however beautiful the pain or the people

i never told him i dreamed the state color of new jersey was white
i believe he was thinking red that night

trapunto drank sherry and trapunto then smiled

red was a color that suited

ONE DAY OF THE QUIET EXCITEMENT

Not quite quiet enough. We remark on the coincidences, the connections. A day of great bravery for me, in small things. I keep meaning to tell you that it is your gift for *sustaining* that you ignore when you say what you love, what you love that others do. You sustained even at first, a delectable white table, I remember the blue silvery shirt I wore that J said was obscene. You wore white, little J a tuxedo. And later or another time you brought the girl and I envied her white skin. So pure, and then with you. Later, years, centuries later, we met her again. And I read D who says he misses K so much and yet he's sleeping already with other women. Death allows this, although life never would. And I worry about your valuables; did you leave them so much in evidence? A little cat scratching at the window every night and she just wants to play when you go to let her in.

I LIKE THE LITTLE ROCKET SHIPS

they satisfy something in me. they are hopeful. they believe they are going higher.

i heard a little song in a dream that went like this:
>look at all the moonlight faces
>moving out of lonely places

i don't know who was singing. might have been me.

i don't feel that i'm getting ready for death
though i should be.
perhaps that's all there is to it.

i am involved in oilcloth, flax linen, redundancies.
i envision the emergency room attendants in fin de siècle costume. fin de which siècle?
the hebrides is not a disease. the small soaps will take care of it.
a few snowflakes is nothing. something beautiful, but nothing at all.
i envision his farm with underground tunnels. the pigs sleep there
but only near the exits.
i understand her wiliness, and she tells good stories. she almost
got arrested in new york
for almost buying an illegal handbag.
these things happen.

her index of affection is high. perhaps she read today
in the new york times
that a cache of civil defense all-purpose survival crackers
was found deep inside the brooklyn bridge
a leftover from the fifties
which is now more than seventy years ago.
of course someone had to taste them and pronounce them "dry."

in the same newspaper a detailed account
of various forgeries. no one knows
which will is real (who will really inherit the earth) or whether
the person who seems to have signed these documents
had a right to.

it was early in the morning and there was surprising weather.
the phone rang.
it was the woman from the flower shop in the dream who said
"i want to send you money to buy yourself a dress."
this could not be permitted, and yet it was. the money had been sitting
in her bank account for years. she considered it at the very same time
she considered not starting a line with a preposition.
the apple blossoms were coming
which meant there would be waxwings. she tried to forget
about the new dress.

there were more things in the plus category but she did not write them down.
she wanted to be very careful.
she was particular about which color blue.

but what does your graphologist say?
she looked at the sky and considered all the options:
"it doesn't make me crazy but
it doesn't turn me on."

IF WE HAD AT LEAST KNOWN THAT ONE BIRD WOULD KEEP US AWAKE FOR THE REST OF THE NIGHT

that might have made a difference,
though it's unlikely. as soon as you think about it
the bird stops singing, and pretty soon you exist
in a "thin place," which someone describes
as a place where off-kilter worlds can speak to each other
as if something just as tangible as air
were all that needed adjustment.

that's where the spirits come through, perfected.
no fillings in their teeth, no rashes, no lice, no
nymphomania. there is about them
a fragrance of sweet lemons—we call them candy ghosts
and for that very reason avoid imbibing
a surfeit of their attraction. all the catholic girl-gods
would find this an absolute treat.

but somewhere between the dinosaurs and the astronauts
i missed the boat.

SELFISHNESS

For the first time in months I felt sane; I had realized my life's work: snowing. I would move up into the atmosphere from thought, I would be born in the minds of children and old people, in the memories of the deaf, who had heard me in a dream. I would harbor the same white innocence children do, the inborn knowledge my death would be swift, clean, honorable. I would never be lonely, never lie, never feel ill-clothed; my speech would be the speech of feathers and my song the song of the pear; my odor would be essence only, mistaken by some for the odor of dew, the odor of temperature, the pungency of air. I would be immune from all dialogue, all puns, every offer.

I would be unique also and need others to complete me, but these others would be decently selected and supplied by the infinite reason who had selected me. Therefore I would not need you. I would not love you. I would not be afraid. For you there would be neither reward nor inconvenience; it would be as if I had not visited your flesh, but had existed as we all exist in that instant in the breaking of an eye where all men and women are snow.

I would live my instant in crystalline perfection, unknown, inexperienced, even hateful in my boreal benignity. There would be the question of god, I suppose. And I would simply deal with that by melting.

IF YOU'RE SLEEPING AND NOT DREAMING, YOU ARE DEAD

i have absorbed the light, almost all
of it, and, although it is not effortless for me,
i will pass it along to you.

this might have happened anyway, who knows,
without the rain dance, the qigong, the meditations, but i must say
that I have done brave things, because these days
everything scares me.

i am broken.
and my fissures have not been repaired with gold.
you can trace your finger along my faults,
and cut your fingers on me if you try.

it was the year your peacock died
"when the insult occurred."
i cannot say which made me sadder. (oh yes i could.)
i consulted a psychic,
but now i am annoyed
at the way she rooted around
in my labyrinths of time.

i'm a bee that is always prospecting
in a flowerless place.

my story is true. i know this is my life
because it died before i was born,
then rose up like a christ.

i shall be cremated in a paper dress
with some of my white ribs showing.
i might request a paper crinoline as well
in case there is dancing.

i might look out from my last bouquet of flames
and cry out like a marigold:
oh ganges take my hand.

THE HOUSE AS A BOX

The house was a box full of boxes and the little girl was choking in the box. The basement was a box with a coal-box in it and the heat came up through a box-shaped grate in the floor. The worst box was a box of dead deer, of deer her father had shot, and there was no need for it. White antlers, black hooves, beautiful fawn-lady faces. The dead deer rode in a box on the hood of the Dodge car and the little girl was good and loved her daddy and loved the deer and the deer was dead and she couldn't make sense of it. Then there was a box of chocolate, of orange-chocolate from the place where the deer was killed, oh dear, and the little girl was unable to make peace with it. Her mother kept the clothespins in a box, the clothes in a box, the clothes washer also. Boxes of cedarsmelling things in the attic and boxes of white lace clothes for boys in the small boxy church. The confessional was a box, as was the father's coffin. A box for the velvet puppets, for the grandmother's necklaces, the violet-colored ferns. Pleased-to-meet-you. All the time the deer hung outside, outside of its box, outside high on the tree near the doghouse (box) and the dog became sad. The little girl was good, she was good and sad, and there was no good reason for all that death and those boxes.

JULY

swarms of dark midges
still twirling in the rain

a bee so heavy with pollen
it bends the blossom down

a circle of sparrows
hopping on dinner street
pecking the tossed tortilla

princess diana and queen elizabeth roses
positioned on opposite sides of the garden
to avoid confrontation

on the front seat of the mazda
an empty wallet
just where you left it full

MING DYNASTY PAJAMAS

the woman in the ming dynasty pajamas is not yours
for the taking

you must wait for her

i have been trying to tell you this for some time

the more you dream about her the less reachable she becomes
as if on some level she knows your dreams
and laughs at them

not unkindly
she is not unkind

but she is practical and she wears pajamas in the daytime
to assert her independence
in fact on some level i believe this is why you like her

inviting her to dinner is fine
but if she says no thank you
say okay
that's fine

don't try to convince her
or even say you'll invite her again

complimenting her taste in clothing is all right too
but don't overdo it
don't make yourself absurd

don't act smarmy
or send chrysanthemums
and don't
take this advice

if it hurts you
after all i am only trying to help

i see you standing there with your heart on your tie
and frankly it makes me sad

MISTAKENLY YOU BELIEVE IT'S ABOUT KINDNESS

1. the soft-eyed man

don't call here again
even if it's somebody's birthday

i'm sorry
i don't mean that
i just want to be alone

i've just established that the song i connect to my meeting with the soft-eyed man
was actually written about another songwriter i connected with the soft-eyed man
in my panoply of the interesting
it makes such sense

the soft-eyed man and the record album with the tropical-colored painting
on the cover
that i left with him
joni something
and the song on that album that i always thought sounded as if it were about him
turns out really (if you believe the gossip) to be about
the songwriter of that song having a love affair with the songwriter of some other
songs and that
second songwriter
also reminded me somehow (perhaps in depth)
of the soft-eyed man

those are the people you carry around with you
is it clear to you now?
what i meant
i mean

i was driving alone this time along route 9 (almost everyone's got one) and came to
the curves in
the road where the horserace used to be
at the sad county fair
the time that miss n and i (who were supposed to be psychic) both
separately and secretly picked the same horse to win and his name was otis

and when the gate was pulled up

in the old-fashioned wooden apparatus our good horse otis
he fell to his knees

well the soft-eyed man and the songwriter(s) interest me still
as does the half-french man carrying the large pot of pink azaleas
those are perhaps the two most interesting and of course they are both dead
(and both had passport problems)

they still speak to me

i don't approve of horse racing

and neither did that good horse otis

orono is in maine and the soft-eyed man is there buried
or so i have read on the internet
he would be amused i know by the recent fact
that houdini's secrets are being revealed
and largely by women

i continually confuse mina and myrna loy
and recently i have learned the word *lanai*
which is of hawaiian origin

2. you could try to get me off the track

but i would not respect you for it
i am not interested in your perky comments
or the details behind them with which you defend your perkiness

i find it makes me tired

life is too short for that
last week i bought
a solar-powered lantern for our garden

which glows long into the morning hours
with a soft orange shine

bracelets of peonies shine below it
ivory in a moonlight they alone emit

these are my beloved peonies
in whom i am well pleased

who give off fragrances uncopiable
and whose leaves breathe on all summer
when the flamboyant blossoms die

3. gone somewhere beyond knowing

i hear you've gone to the doctor
once again
only to be told there's nothing really wrong
it's a moral problem
or a problem of your dreams
you have an unfortunate relationship
with your bedside table
which you have given a woman's name
bianca you call her
and it seems you cannot be a friend
to anyone who befriends you
since bianca is very jealous of your glances
and does not want them pausing indiscreetly on others

you wear what you wear
but it does not flatter
and finally
after all these years
i must refuse to dress you

4. unlooked-for muscular weakness

even the eyes will not focus
when fatigue is so dense
mistakenly you believe it's all about kindness
or the lack thereof

that a cold embrace on a rainy day
abolishes the past or even the future

that the salamander fooling around
in the crook of the exposed root of the swampland tree
has got your number

5. gentle horse's eye

they are so tall and large and just because
they can't sit in chairs
they're not appreciated

a horse's gentle eye is bigger than yours
brighter

the horse is not picking her words for any purpose
but to tell you something

when the child was mild
she was like this horse

not now she's not
and she sits in her chair
and chooses her words for reasons
she can't understand

IN THE OTHER HOUSE IT WAS BOTH COLDER
AND HOTTER

Here we have better insulation.
Would you mind if I cuddled up a little?

I could tell you my dreams.

Last night was pretty funny with all those newspapers.
Some of them had interviews with me in which I said things as if I knew what I was thinking
all the time. You know that's not true.
Like the way you'll sometimes ask me what I'm thinking and I'll say
I don't know (much
to your consternation because you think
I'm trying to be evasive),
but the truth is I *don't* know or don't
know
in the way that would satisfy you. I'm streaming.

I'm going from thought to thought so fast it's a flurried unpunctuated blur
and really it doesn't bother me: it's comfortable
and I only get uncomfortable when somebody asks me about it and I'm surprised
out of it. Not that you shouldn't ask.

Anyway the newspapers in that dream were full
of black-and-white photographs too
and one of the photos was captioned "Experience." It showed
a forsythia bush (you could tell even in black-and-white),
a small rabbit, a canvas lounge chair (the old-fashioned type
with cut-outs and white
seam binding), and in the sky over the lounge chair you could just make out
a twin-engined plane. Inside the plane (you could not see this) were two men

one in a baseball cap,
one in a tizzy.

They were looking down with binoculars expecting to see the chair inhabited
by a beautiful girl.
They could only see the rabbit.

What they did not know was that the girl was hiding in the long skirts of the forsythia bush.

You know that now.

NO MAIL TODAY,

not even a flyer. it's not a holiday
yet we've been forgotten
here on this visible street
where neighbors park half on their lawn
and half on ours. no reason

i dropped a needle on the rug
and cannot see it; no reason

a moth has fallen
into the dish of oil
i put out for the bread, and floats
among the spices
like a miniature sailboat upset
by miniature weather. i heard
some talk of you and what you said.

i watched as a splinter, lodged painlessly for years,
emerged from under my nail
with a drop of antique blood and a shot of pleasure. now

i won't need the needle anymore; this job
is done. the mail might just as well have come.
the day is seamed together.

MY TRIP TO ICELAND

people like you i'm not sure why

today is like getting on one of those automatic conveyor-belt trains in an airport
where all the stations look exactly the same and you can't tell if you're coming or
going
one time in newark i rode the thing several times around before getting oriented
and no one could help me as they were all likewise confused

we kept him in a sunny terrarium because he couldn't swim
pebbles the turtle boy
who usually walked backwards because his feet were floppy

people put up with you kindly
even when you're looking over their shoulders
but they shouldn't do that

it will not improve your character

when i got on the ship there was trouble in the hold
a man with an orange shirt was smoking dope with the deckhands
people with wide straw hats were drinking martinis almost everywhere
i was anxious and sent turtle boy a postcard
but was worried that it wouldn't be mailed till the ship docked in iceland
five years from now

by that time pebbles might be all grown up

on the ship there are no arrangements for library usage
or *etch-a-sketch* meditations
horrendously people throw sweaters over their shoulders
as if they are in old movies
and have no taste
they lounge in deckchairs with their white limbs lolling
using expressions like "in the offing" and
"on the same page"

i say they are "all a-flutter"
and probably they won't change

THE WOMAN WHO COULD SEE EVERYTHING BUT FACES

one of my cats was snoring.

i had a dream in which everything i said
was interesting

but when i woke up it was gone
of course.
i was so involved

with the mechanics of fingers
i could see nothing, or rather
i could see everything
but faces

so if i were to recognize you
upon our second meeting
it would likely be from your voice
or the scent of lavender on your ear
or that rough spot flaking off

from your wrist.
the left one. the right one
is perfectly smooth. i want
black-framed eyeglasses but i don't
look good in them. i want dr. phil
to stop talking

about possibilities. i want
the wood-duck in our brook
to come have some wine with us
at midnight. i am not serious; i have deep respect
for ducks. i want to accept
my need for rapport with birds
and the strange feel of their sinewy necks

beneath their feathers. the day that i was shattered
i was born. i began to wear black

and pretend to be holy. i dipped my fingers
into the chilly fieldstone crock. i did feel good about it
however. the thin high air
walking home from church
on mornings when no one else was about.

but i should have been protected.

IT SEEMS AS IF A COMBINATION OF CONSONANTS AND VOWELS IS BEST

I want you to know the best of me. I will put on my capital letters. I will strip my
body of all its pretence. I will spell velvet
with two v's. In the morning of the story I will shave the thistles
from the artichoke heads
and pull you out into mist and northern sun. I feel
a little cold, that's all.

All the dishes in the world have been broken.
even the wooden ones. There is nothing you can do,
nothing I can do for you. Live in as many worlds as you can. Become
the very mirror, so you can plainly see.

On the first begonia of every month
thoughts will be withdrawn from your account
without your knowledge.

There will be other lives, and we will live them.
This sorrow, as we call it, will become a broken globe.

CLAIRVOYANCE

those we hate most
those apples hitting the tin garage roof

dead of night

knowing why doesn't help

the grocery store samples lady with her hotplate

zoom in on that, would you?
her fierce pride in the sliced fritters
first time i saw her i knew

the porch in childhood
a stiff white christmas tree with blue lights
some carry that hideous pallor all their lives

ELEVATOR GOSSIP

If the story has no appeal,
it is because the characters have effused in the darkness.
There is a removal and a half-removal,
a slight weather in the way she pauses
as if waiting only
to take a drink from the fountain.
She turns so lightly on her heel
and draws the fleece collar practically upwards.
Oh one would think her innocent of knowing
the smallest thing about the stolen objects.

I don't want to hear them laughing about you,
although they are laughing kindly.
The forward edge of the tongue is so sensitive
to every type of sugar and salt.
(When that evening the monster was sighted again
only the old woman in woolen trousers gave it refreshment.)

The pearl-grey days are best, the dampness needed.
If the story has no appeal
it is because the characters have eliminated darkness.
It is because in the end I refused him a pin:
I had to. Imagine the shame in what I heard.
Imagine a day like this grey without sound,
a frail tableau of the smallest birds,
an animal on the rocks, pulse tightened.
One can almost feel its lovely tongue.

Diane Wald has published more than 250 poems in literary magazines since 1966. She the recipient of a two-year fellowship in poetry from the Fine Arts Work Center in Provincetown and has been awarded the Grolier Poetry Prize, The Denny Award, The Open Voice Award, and the Anne Halley Award. She also received a state grant from the Artists Foundation (Massachusetts Council on the Arts). She has published four print chapbooks (*Target of Roses* from Grande Ronde Press, *My Hat That Was Dreaming* from White Fields Press, *Double Mirror* from Runaway Spoon Press, and *Faustinetta, Gegenschein, Trapunto* from Cervena Barva Press) and won the Green Lake Chapbook Award from Owl Creek Press. An electronic chapbook (*Improvisations on Titles of Works by Jean Dubuffet*) appears on the Mudlark website. Her book Lucid Suitcase was published by Red Hen Press in 1999 and her second book, *The Yellow Hotel*, was published by Verse Press in the fall of 2002. *Wonderbender*, her third collection, was published by 1913 Press in 2011. Her novel *Gillyflower* was published in April 2019 by She Writes Press, and won first place in the novella category from the Next Generation Indie Book Awards, first place in the novella category from American Book Fest, and a bronze medal from Reader's Favorite. A novel, *My Famous Brain*, is forthcoming in October 2021 from She Writes Press.

www.ingramcontent.com/pod-product-compliance
Lightning Source LLC
Chambersburg PA
CBHW021156090426
42740CB00008B/1122